Divorce Tactics for Women that Work

Protect Yourself Emotionally, Physically and Financially

Jane Wymer

Divorce isn't pleasant in the best of circumstances, but even worse when betrayal, resentment, bitterness or anger is added into the mix. This book is dedicated to women to realistically prepare them for the many scenario's that can play out during a divorce.

Copyright Act of 1976, the scanning, uploading and electronic sharing of any part of this book without the explicit written consent or permission of the publisher constitutes unlawful piracy and the theft of intellectual property.

If you would like to use material or content from this book (other than for review purposes), prior written permission must be obtained from the publisher.

You can contact the publishing company at admin@speedypublishing.com. Thank you for not infringing on the author's rights.

Speedy Publishing LLC (c) 2014
40 E. Main St., #1156
Newark, DE 19711
www.speedypublishing.co

Ordering Information:
Quantity sales; Special discounts are available on quantity purchases by corporations, associations, and others. For details, contact the "Special Sales Department" at the address above.

This is a reprint book.

Manufactured in the United States of America

Table of Contents

Publisher's Notes i

Chapter 1: No-One Ever Plans on Divorce 1

Chapter 2: Divorce - The Final Event of Your Marriage 4

Chapter 3: Never Underestimate The Rage of an Ex 7

Chapter 4: Protecting Yourself with Security Measures 12

Chapter 5: More Security Tips 15

Chapter 6: Learn Art of Negotiation 19

Chapter 7: Rules to Follow During the Divorce Process 21

Chapter 8: The Reasons Why People Get Divorced 30

Chapter 9: How To Gain The Upper Hand During the Divorce Process 35

Chapter 10: Conclusion 44

Meet the Author 46

More Books by Jane Wymer 48

Publisher's Notes

Disclaimer

This publication is intended to provide helpful and informative material. It is not intended to diagnose, treat, cure, or prevent any health problem or condition, nor is intended to replace the advice of a physician. No action should be taken solely on the contents of this book. Always consult your physician or qualified health-care professional on any matters regarding your health and before adopting any suggestions in this book or drawing inferences from it.

The author and publisher specifically disclaim all responsibility for any liability, loss or risk, personal or otherwise, which is incurred as a consequence, directly or indirectly, from the use or application of any contents of this book.

Any and all product names referenced within this book are the trademarks of their respective owners. None of these owners have sponsored, authorized, endorsed, or approved this book.

Always read all information provided by the manufacturers' product labels before using their products. The author and publisher are not responsible for claims made by manufacturers.

Print Edition 2014

Chapter 1: No-One Ever Plans on Divorce

You didn't walk down the aisle with the intention of being divorced. You chose your mate because you thought it was with the understanding of being together all your lives. However sometimes things just don't work out and the only way to be free of an unhappy relationship or marriage is the final act of divorce.

Marriage and Divorce Statistics

In the United States these are the latest figures regarding marriage and divorce according to the US Census Bureau dated 2009.

Marriage Rate = 6.8 per 1,000 for the total population. Number of Marriages: 2,096,000. Divorce Rate = 3.6 per 1,000 populations

(There were 44 reporting States and Washington D.C.) From these figures it seems for every marriage there was also half the amount of divorces. Those are some pretty high statistics.

Domestic Abuse

Statistics say that one in four women will Experience domestic violence at some point in their lives. One in 3 women will fall victim to a homicide by a spouse or partner through domestic violence. Men in same sex relationships will also be at higher risks of experiencing abuse. Approximately 3 million children will witness domestic violence in their home every year in the USA.

The figures above are not only frightening but an ugly realty of what actually can happen in divorce. Staying alert with an Ex-partner, or Ex-husband can be one of the smartest moves to make. I'm not saying to become fearful but rather be on alert for certain patterns in behavior, fits of anger, depression and other factors that can trigger huge changes through divorce.

People can change dramatically when going through the divorce process and the person we always thought we knew, can turn into someone dark and sometimes sinister.

Of course there are other factors that make divorce even more stressful like lawyers, counselors, custody of the children and the split of finances. People will more than likely change with the ups and downs of the divorce process, which is something most of us Expect. However, most of us are never ready for the ugly and sometimes evil side of an Ex that may come out through the divorce process.

Let this guide be a source for information related to awareness and proactive defense if needed. The goal of this book is help you through the rocky road of divorce and arm yourself with Guerilla Warfare Tactics that may arise to help in the emotional, physical and financial protection defense of you, your children and your home.

"If there is an underlying relationship between domestic violence and divorce regime, we would Expect to observe changing violence propensities in the treatment group relative to the controls. Because the survey universe consists only of couples living in a conjugal unit, we are limited to analyzing rates of domestic violence within intact marriages. Crime victimization survey data both lack state identifiers and are not available for the relevant time period. Police reports suffer both from serious problems of under-reporting and, more importantly, changes in social norms regarding reporting over the relevant time period." Murray A. Straus and Richard J. Gelles, quote from "Physical Violence in American Families". The 1976 and 1985 surveys are ICPSR studies 9211 and 7733, respectively.

Chapter 2: Divorce - The Final Event of Your Marriage

Realize that divorce is the final act in your marriage. Millions of people end up going through divorce and sadly many of them, never recover. Sure, they may be alive but they are former shells of what they once were.

You can eventually benefit and grow strong but only if you have the strength, family and friends to rally around you. Sometimes this process can take years.

Divorce can rob us of our dignity, wealth and security. Even though it is necessary sometimes, there is always a price for it. Pay attention to what is just, fair and things what will benefit you.

It's not ok to allow the soon to be Ex to tell you that "I'm taking this and I will leave you that if the split is 70 /30 in favor of them or vice versa."

Divorce is a terrible thing. It fills you with anger, resentment and deep pain. You want the other party to suffer for the betrayal. You actually begin to plot another human being's suffering. Didn't you used to love him? So how can you dislike them so much that you want them to suffer?

You need to learn how to let go of the pain right way. Holding onto hate and anger will prevent you from growing happy and healthy. Your life can degenerate into a "fatal Attraction" scenario that can end up costing you deep and lasting pain. Divorce is not fashionable even though statistics tells us otherwise.

I want to encourage you to move into a happier place. Will it be easy? NO! Can you conquer your fears and misgivings? Of course, but then some of you might also need someone to help you through this. Like a wounded man on the battlefield, your chances of survival double if there is a friend to help carry you out of the trenches.

Life will always have its challenges and that old theory "no pain no gain" comes to mind here. However, this is what helps us to build character, learn from our choices and grow to be healthier and stronger. Your reactions to these challenges either teach you or make you withdraw in pain. What will your choice be?

Knowing the truth sets you free, acting upon it, is necessary for those around you to realize that you will no longer be the dirt beneath someone else's feet, or the person who is afraid to speak up in the right way, not just react to it.

Grow strong, be happy and choose a path that will benefit others not just you. You know you can achieve this, by proving to yourself that you are worthy and will no longer think otherwise.

Chapter 3: Never Underestimate The Rage of an Ex

In our society there are people that will never play fair. This book was put together because quite frankly, some people are monsters and you need relevant information to protect yourself and your family from them.

Your Ex might not have been capable of unspeakable acts in the past but statistics show that during divorce this can quickly change.

Will your Ex move on with his life or will he become one of those people who can never let it go? Will he become obsessed with rage and anger seeking to hurt you?

Sometimes this means the worst possible outcome. Here is where you must get involved to protect yourself, your children, your home, your life and stand guard ready to defend yourself. It is an attitude of power.

But how? How does any person truly protect themselves?

Learn from those who have gone down this dark road and lived to tell the tale.

The information in this book can literally save your peace of mind, your finances and maybe even your life.

There are evil people in the world. Could your Ex become one or maybe he already is? No matter how hard you try to be civil sometimes, in the end, their rage and anger could end up endangering your life.

Some people are truly capable of becoming psychopaths and only need the right stimulus or trigger. Divorce can be the straw that broke the camel's back and cause the Ex to become a real threat.

"The truth is that we are all monsters just beneath our social masks waiting for the right moment to consume and destroy."

~ Unknown Author

We are going to explore the darker area of people's behavior, because it is important to understand how everyone is capable of becoming a Dr. Jekyll and Mr. Hyde.

A survey of men, who were in the process of divorcing, were asked what their darkest fantasy was and if they could get away with it what they might do to their former wife. The answers are horrifying.

Brace yourself; these are actual statements of men involved in divorce: "I'd like to slowly strangle the bitch and watch the color run from her face!"

"Rape her, cut her throat and leave her in the woods."

"I want to tie up the %@$# and hang her from a tree to die in slow agony."

"Yeah tell that @ucking whore I'm gonna kill her someday."

"She will never get away from me. Someday I'm sure she will die (by my hand)."

These statements varied in intensity—and there were more, some much more graphic. Sorry to say that these statements were from cases where actual interviews took place.

Surprisingly enough some of those above quotes were from men who were higher educated and in a seething rage about getting divorced. Men view divorce as a gladiatorial confrontation – a winner take all. It is hardwired in their behavior sometimes. They believe that it is all or nothing.

The majority of men who were interviewed all wanted to get even with their Ex and a majority were working on ways to make the woman pay dearly in some form or another. Even if it wasn't physical violence it certainly would be through other means.

Almost ALL of the men surveyed were plotting to deeply hurt their former spouse. For this reason alone you need to understand that you have to be ready.

Later we will cover non-threatening ways for you to try and get your Ex to dissipate his anger so he does not turn his rage towards you. However, these tactics do not always work.

Anger, rage and revenge that is brought on by a divorce needs to be acknowledged and taken seriously. Something you must never do is under estimate your Ex during a divorce.

Assuming you have exhausted every way to reconcile your marriage, at some point you need to approach your Ex and beg him to keep the divorce civil, especially if you have children.

Despite the fact that advocacy groups like NOW have worked for two decades to halt the epidemic of gender-based violence and sexual assault, the numbers are still shocking.

For example, in 2005, 1,181 women were murdered by an intimate partner. That's an average of three women every day. Of all the women murdered in the U.S., about one-third was killed by an intimate partner.

These predatory people do not warrant the title of "human". Our prisons are filled with people who have, sometimes horrifically, murdered their Ex.

Had any of these women had a plan (studies show that most did not) they may have survived. No one likes to believe that someone you were married to and loved could ever do this. Yet every year over 1,000 women are often brutally slain by former intimate partners.

Are you paying attention? Some of you already know exactly what your Ex is capable of.

Many of the tactics in this book discuss ways to "Detect & Protect."

No plan is foolproof but if you follow the tactics outlined in this book, the advantage is yours. These tactics are grouped in basic levels of protection that anyone can do. A great deal of time was spent interviewing security Experts to provide this information. If your situation is extremely bad you might consider hiring a professional to protect you.

Chapter 4: Protecting Yourself with Security Measures

Security Basics:

Barriers – are your first line of defense between you and your adversary. There are several ways you can create barriers.

Some barriers are psychological in nature and physical as well. For example; fencing, camera's and alarm systems are both physical and psychological barriers.

Look into alarming your home. Systems vary in price and some can be installed by the homeowner. Do some research online and you will be surprised to find systems that are affordable. If you think you can't afford an alarm system then consider this: what is your life worth?

Alarm systems do more than just make noise. Modern monitoring services can detect intruders, detect open doors, open windows, fire, carbon monoxide, even water and smoke damage. They can instantly alert the police, call you if you are away from your home or protected area the instant an intruder breaks in (possibly saving your life) contact fire department and ambulance even if you can't.

The panic button features or motion detection that is set after you go to bed will allow you to sleep relatively peacefully. Cheap and effective you should first implement this because security systems work well to frighten off intruders as well and will discourage theft or vandalism of your property.

If you live in an apartment, you can do a few things to protect yourself. Doorjamb alarms emit 125 DB of ear splitting sound if it is moved touched, stepped on or a door is opened even a little on it.

Cheap insurance and the noise generated will tell your assailant that you know they are trying to break in your premises. Similar alarms exist for windows and these alarms are all under 20 dollars.

Many are under fifteen dollars and can be wired to a main alarm set up to trigger and call you, the police and even give an audible warning that an intruder can hear, "Warning you have been detected and the police have been called!" Studies have determined that criminals will retreat and flee when challenged with an audible deterrent.

Apartment living can be adapted for wireless personal alarm systems that consists of a main control unit with a 105 dB alarm, one door/window sensor, one motion detector sensor and a remote control with panic button.

Please take physical security and barriers seriously. Implement security measures to prevent harm versus installing security measures out of fear after something bad has happened. Implementing security is affordable and capable of protecting you, your property and allows you to sleep better at night.

Chapter 5: More Security Tips

Purchasing homeowners insurance or renter's insurance is a good idea for a couple of reasons.

Why Insurance?

Imagine a fire, theft or burglary. If your Ex decides you have something he wants or doesn't want you to have, a vengeful house fire could happen. It is also smart to protect yourself and such insurance like renters is effective. Store your most expensive items, documents in a safety deposit box or fake storage container (hollowed out book, fake safe in plain sight). You should always keep documents (like divorce papers, passports, birth certificates and restraining orders) and valuables in a safety deposit box away from the premises.

Research wireless and motion infra-red cameras (very affordable kits exist for a few hundred dollars or less) that can record, broadcast and be moved easily to any location and even be disguised to look like other items.

Make sure every camera you purchase or safety system can produce date and time stamps. It will be a lifesaver in a court room if need be.

Lock doors and windows every time you leave the house and when you are home as well. I know it sounds simple but most people do not lock their doors during the day when they are home. You must lock your doors at all times (barrier principle).

Join neighborhood watch or start one – One of the most overlooked strategies for self-protection and it costs nothing. Yet even a watchful neighbor (especially older people would love something to do like this) can prevent a crime. Extra eyes are critical – and even if you don't find many people to be part of this kind of organization you can post flyers all over where you live saying this community is a neighborhood watch community.

Make sure you post these flyers everywhere where you live and surrounding your neighborhood from every way your Ex might travel to get to your home. This kind of psychological alerting to would be thieves (and angry Ex's) could deter them from committing crimes against you.

What if you simply can't afford an alarm system?

Here is cheap deterrence for a few dollars – Amazon sells alarm stickers. Place these security stickers on the windows of your home or property to announce to would-be intruders that your property is protected by an alarm system.

Thieves are looking for the easiest home or car to burglarize. The presence of these stickers can cause them to pass by your property in search of an easier target. These stickers can be a deterrent only if you are the only person who knows there is no alarm system. If kids, family or friends leak to your Ex that there is no system, your stickers are worthless.

Portable Concealed Self Protection

Non-lethal protection is your best bet. Why? Most states legally allow you to carry things like mace, pepper spray, stun guns and similar protection devices.

The absolute best protection device is something you keep on your person all the times even when you sleep; always ready to defend yourself. A direct spray into an assailant's face will more than likely allow you to get away.

What About Firearms?

Guns are an absolute weapon of final choice. Gun ownership for self-defense is a personal choice. Please understand that weapons of this magnitude require training, safe handling and absolute control for using it – as well as knowledge of the law so that your self-defense does not end up as you going to prison for a very long time or worse yet, a victim of your own weapon.

Use of mace, stun guns or non-lethal defense shows you had no intent of killing someone – and important consideration if you ever end up in court. Discharging a firearm could end with a person dead and you having to live with that for the rest of your life.

A Better Tactic

Flee To a Safe room or safe location –even if you live in an apartment you can set up a place (like in the back of your closet) where if any of your alarms go off – you immediately flee to. In this location are implements of self–defense and a communication device.

Let's face facts, even though you may have a restraining order on your Ex what are the chances that the police will be at your residence in time, if they decide to break into your home?

In some cases the police are so overwhelmed now that unless there is a murder involved you are not on the top of their list. So you have to make plans for the just in case scenario's.

CHAPTER 6: LEARN ART OF NEGOTIATION

Learning to be clever in the negotiation practices in the middle of a divorce can be a huge tipping point in your favor. While the Ex may become angry or emotional across the table in front of lawyers, you have to learn to become almost stoic in your behavior and thinking.

There is a speaker in the USA called Roger Dawson. He is one of the best when it comes to negotiating deals. Roger holds seminars where he teaches people how to become better at this art too. Success magazine called him "America's Premier Business Negotiator."

When you go through divorce it defiantly becomes like a business negotiation, so there is a point as to why we are using Roger as an example of becoming incredibly smart at negotiation.

Too many times we involve our personal feelings and emotions into our divorces and while that is completely understandable it is not in your best interest. If you can look at your divorce situation like a business deal gone badly, you would be much better off. Take the emotion out of the picture for time being and just get what is owed to you!

Chapter 7: Rules to Follow During the Divorce Process

Rule: Plan what you are going to do FIRST and Foremost.

I can't stress this enough. Too many people just leave with no outlets or systems set in place to help them when in the middle of a divorce.

Sometimes you have no recourse but to leave in abusive situations, and that is completely understandable. The safest thing for you is to be gone if there is abuse of any kind.

Make sure the new environment you move to is less stressful so that you can start to plan for the success of your part in the divorce. Start with a check list of what you want to achieve, your new living arrangements, the finances and anything else that needs to be discussed and shared. Stick with the list; do not be persuaded to lower your list standards by your Ex or deviate from your goals.

Rule: Just because you don't have any money doesn't mean you cannot get a divorce.

Legal Aid has some restrictions on it you will need to check them out. Emotional abuse is not really something they will help you with.

However if you are being physically abused, you may be able to get help. Much of this kind of help is based on your income and the severity of the case in question.

Women's Shelters are excellent sources of Information too. Get a temporary custody order of your children first if you believe yourself to be the better parent. This will give you more bargaining power in the court room if you have put this procedure in place right from the start. Get a restraining order If you are being harassed, physically hurt, or are fearful for you safety and well-being.

You will need the previous year's joint tax paperwork that was filed with the IRS. Most legal documents want to see your and the husbands income. Keep pay stubs if you have them as well.

Social Security cards and all other forms of Identification need to be kept handy at all times. You can and are very capable of doing your own divorce if your funds are very limited.

Rule: Your financial status should be changed out ASAP

You need money, bank account access and other very important things. Get a personal savings or checking account with only your name on it before you leave your husband. If you are getting direct deposit into your joint checking account change it into your personal checking account ASAP.

As long as you have a joint checking account your spouse can take every last penny out of the account and there is nothing legally you can do about it. Play it safe and have your accounts set up quickly to protect your own interests.

Assets like your home, land, property, cars and IRA's will need to be completed on your financial paperwork to the court when dividing legally.

You will need to take all of this information to the court house with you when filing for the divorce paperwork. Make at least three copies of everything, this will save you time, energy and frustration when going to the courthouse.

Rule: Keep a daily journal and write everything down in it.

Phone calls to the partner/spouse, dates, times, things said to each other and threats made. This can be a real lifesaver. Understand this, the more evidence you have the more power you will have in court. Don't get mad, get even, the sneaky way.

Journals are often used in court hearings as evidence. If you are constantly arguing then write down everything that is said. Words said can be used in a court room with a journal that is filled with notes. The Judge may ask to see your journal when you are in court.

Don't underestimate the importance of a well-documented journal. A journal full of times, dates, places, threats and statements looks really good to a judge.

Rule: Research the divorce/filing procedures for your county.

Get as much information as you can by searching your local county courthouse online. The majority of county websites have a wealth of resources, support groups, legal advice, paperwork and government agencies that may be able to help you. Each county and state have paperwork you can download and fill out on your own. There are assistants and volunteers that offer you their time and services in filing legal papers correctly. Make an appointment with them. Your local courthouse should be able to put you in touch with these people.

Rule: Make a list of your Ex's bad habits. Write down things like; gambling, smoking, drugs, alcohol, on-line dating, etc. Do strip clubs and porn sites occupy your Ex's time and money? Keep your ears and eyes open.

Friends, relatives, and even your children may spill the goodies about your spouse. You have to be alert, careful and above all stay calm. Don't sink to the level of the dirty mess you are searching for. Do not harass and pester the kids about daddy. Do not pick your family friends brains either. If your kids accidently mention something worthwhile, write it in your journal.

If a family friend volunteers information, write it down. Try and stay dignified at all times and never try to deceive other people. This annoys your friends and they may end up speaking against you.

Rule: Never jump at the first offer made to you.

Remember the art of negotiation! Never give in too soon or this will give the other party power from the get go. Being able to hold out for more also shows that you are not a push over and you will no longer tolerate anyone being able to dictate what they think you are entitled too. If the soon to be Ex becomes annoyed because you have refused to give into their whims, then this behavior is on them. You just walk away and remain strong.

Rule: Ask for more than you actually expect to get.

This will give you room to negotiate in the long run. Your first offer should actually be fairly unreasonable. As a matter of fact it should be laughable. This kind of offer will make the other party re-think their strategy too.

Have a final goal in mind of where you want to be and write it down. Get it into your head that you will only negotiate up to that point. You will not go below the acceptance point. Place this goal in a place where you can see it like the refrigerator or a mirror as the psychological battle is already fought in your head.

Rule: Avoid Confrontation in your negotiating

There is nothing worse than seeing two people screaming at each other in a public place. It is demeaning and very childish. It is not good in building character either. Especially if you are trying to impress the Judge and show him or her that you are the bigger person.

Let the Ex throw their temper tantrums while you just walk away in silence from them. Actually silence is a great teacher of people's behavior. When they act like a child, don't treat them like a child, just walk away, completely silent. Just keep going and don't you dare turn around or the other party wins.

Rule: Use all your power and means available to you.

If you give someone an inch they will usually take a mile. Understand you are in this divorce because you are tired of the same old situation. You are here to win-period!

If you allow the other party to gain control the first time, you may as well give it up, right there. The more you learn about the legal system, negotiations, resources available to you and even a little psychology will save you headaches, time and sanity.

Rule: Do not buy into the emotional and verbal blackmail control babble.

This kind of verbal diarrhea is why you are sitting in the court room to begin with. I thought you were sick of it? The new woman is empowered so act like it. Stop giving your power, time and energy to this kind of abuse.

Children are always used as emotional pawns in these types of games. As long as you do not say one unkind word in front of your children about their father, then your kids will figure things out on their own.

Understand your kids are much smarter than your spouse wants you to think they are. Tell the Ex that you do not want to discuss the children with him or her unless it is important.

The Ex will nearly always try and use the kids as an emotional crutch to you, if you let them. You are supposed to be the bigger person. The soon to be Ex knows what buttons to push to raise your temper too.

Stay Calm. Change the subject quickly and ask "Is there is anything else?" before you leave or hang up. They will figure out really quickly that you are not buying it anymore.

Question: If one parent is constantly running the other parent down to the children, who do you think your kids will run too?

Answer: The opposite parent who is not running their mouth all the time, that's who.

Rule: Stay Calm, Poised and Very Together At All Times.

This cannot be stressed enough especially when a situation can easily become volatile with face to face contact with the Ex. If you understand there are triggers to set you or the Ex off, then back off and become silent and remove yourself from the situation. Conversations over the telephone need to be calm and almost relaxed, to avoid shouting matches and constant aggravation.

Do not allow the new girlfriend to control your life. You are not here to have your feathers ruffled by the new love. This person is not your mother or father. Their opinions about you or the divorce have no relevance in your life. It is not any of their business what is happening in the divorce.

She is not your children's parent and her opinion about your parenting skills is just another way to rile you up. Laugh at her and tell her to mind her own business and then zip it. Your Ex is counting on agitating you but if you remain calm, it throws a huge monkey wrench into the plans.

Calm stoic like behavior, drives people who want to rile others up, into a state of confusion and in the long run it gives you the upper hand.

Did you ever consider that the Ex might actually be counting on you getting upset with the new love? Actually it may have been a planned attack to see how far you will go.

Some Ex's especially some male's relish the idea of having two women fighting over them; don't fall for the games and manipulation.

What is the old saying "What goes around comes around?" Remember that it will serve you well.

CHAPTER 8: THE REASONS WHY PEOPLE GET DIVORCED

Two of the biggest problems most people face in today's society related to divorce, is a lack of commitment towards their marriage and infidelity.

Commitment may be lacking in one of the partners because the marriage "happened" and they were not really in love. Maybe the wife was pregnant and the husband just did the right thing to keep the peace within the families. This partner may have felt forced in the marriage and now they are trapped, angry, resentful and bored.

Spouses who are unhappy will not be loyal to their partners.

Lack of communication between spouses

Without communication no relationship can work. Keeping your resentments simmering within you is very unhealthy. Your partner does not know what is happening with you, so this is likely to create distance between both of you. An explosive boiling point is the usual result of no communication as one partner eventually loses it on the other.

Abandonment, Alcohol Addiction, Substance Abuse

When one of the partners deserts their spouse for a certain time or an indefinite period divorce emerges as the answer. This can even be in the form of spending excessive amounts of time at the local bar. Sitting in the house getting drunk or under the influence of drugs will ultimately cause the relationship to fail too. If one person is doing the drugs and the other is not, there is really not that much the relationship has going for it. The two people are obviously at different ends of the spectrum.

Physical Abuse, Sexual Abuse and Emotional Abuse

These types of abuses are not uncommon and tolerating them is never acceptable. A spouse who loves themselves would not put up with such abuses on his family or loved one.

It is not uncommon to see the abused victim protect their abusive spouse and even make excuses for the bruises or marks on their bodies. The fact is once you realize the extent of the control in your relationship; the decision can only be one of two choices.

Stay and take the abuse or leave and live your life free of abuse.

Inability to manage or resolve conflict

Lack of maturity disables people to manage conflicts and handle personality differences. Young people/teenagers getting married have less of a chance because they do not have enough life Experiences to base their lives on. Sometimes this is because of a pregnancy and the two teenagers feel it is better for their child to be married. Usually within a few years they are divorced because of the strain of raising children as no more than children themselves.

Differences in Personal and Career Goals

People who live together before marriage have higher rates of divorce than people who didn't.

Distance enters the marriage and the relationship broadens to the point of complete breakdown. Sometimes the conflict is about jealousy as one spouse is bent on competing with the other over a job or career.

Different expectations about household tasks and financial problems. Financial problems can be a major source for problems in a marriage. One partner may feel they carry more of the load and take their frustrations out on the wife or husband. In these cases love can become sour quickly. Feelings of frustration and an inability to change the situation becomes more dominant in the partner taking the load.

Intellectual Inflexibility

Intellectual incompatibility creates misunderstandings. The smarter person feels frustrated, while the less intelligent partner is mad about not reaching the same level, as the other one. The pair makes each other miserable with snide remarks, comments that maybe someone is a grunt at their job while the other is an executive.

Mental Instability or Mental Illness

Sometimes when the spouse becomes deeply depressed the partner may not understand this. It is too frustrating and aggravating for the other person to accept. Also mental illness does not allow space for normal communication between spouses.

Many times after a child is born the wife may go through a depression that seems to take forever to get over and the husband becomes frustrated with her lack of desire to be intimate and say things to her like "You never used to be like this." The wife may be tired, overwhelmed and depressed with the new baby. Lack of understanding and comforting can cause a huge rift in the marriage.

Religious beliefs, cultural and lifestyle differences

Cultural views will eventually clash unless we learn to adapt. Western and Eastern cultures can make a relationship difficult to meld.

The new religion was not what you were married into. The partner may not accept this new religion or even try to understand it. They are feeling left out, angry and betrayed.

When people have valid reasons to divorce, they often know when the marriage it has played itself out. After all, there is no point in hanging on to a person if you can no longer live together.

When it's time to move on, move on!

CHAPTER 9: HOW TO GAIN THE UPPER HAND DURING THE DIVORCE PROCESS

Here are eight factors that give YOU Power over People and your Situation:

1. Legitimate and Legal

Get to know the legal system in your state and county like the back of your hand. Custody situations need to be always handled with care. Know the visitation rights of the other parent.

- If you are looking for total custody then you have to have a good reason. Abuse and neglect could be the reason, and then you will need proof to back this up.
- Take pictures of your kids before they go off to visit their father or other partner.

- When they come back to you, look at them and their bodies. If there are bruises on their body take more pictures that day.
- Do not pick up the phone and start screaming at your EX about the marks on your child's body.
- Instead, record and tape all conversations with your spouse over these marks in a controlled and civil manner. It will go better for you in the court room.
- NEVER question your own children without a witness present, find a neighbor if you have to. You can use this as a testimony in court and it also shows other people how much of a better parent you are.
- A Judge may order your children have a session with a court appointed Psychologist. You do not want to implant your own thoughts into your child's head. This will go against you. Your child will speak if you have been loving and honest with them.
- Explain to your child, that there is nothing to be afraid of. You will always be here to protect them. Just tell the truth, is all you can ask them to do.

2. Coercive and Persuasive

By knowing the legal system you will be able to persuade not only the Judge but possibly your spouse as to your power and rights as well.

Especially in the custody cases as I have mentioned above.

The court will decide based on the child's interview what is best in their opinion. If you have taken all the above steps we suggest, I assure you that the Custody situation should not be a problem. Remember the Judge wants a record of everything. The more evidence the better you are off.

3. Reverent (Worshipped) or Admired

Even though your spouse may despise you for continually outsmarting him or her in the divorce, let me tell you something, eventually they will respect you.

Never again will they try and pull numerous lies or manipulation on you. You are now too smart for any of that old garbage. Other people and family members who never thought; "You had it in you either," will now admire your strength and character in taking charge of your life on your own.

4. Charisma and Personality

Do not go into the court room looking and feeling like a mouse.

Do you really think you have gained power over your spouse or anyone, looking this way?

What will the Judge think of you?

I can tell you now; people who walk into a court room with their head held high and dressing like a professional get the judge's attention. In their view, you make a good mother, a responsible adult and a take charge person.

Your spouse is going to look at you as well.

Do you know what they are going to think? "Wow, she looks great!"

Inside his head is spinning because you have now just gained the upper hand. You never looked this good before and he will not be able to believe the change in you.

This is the message you are trying to get across to everyone; you want the soon to be Ex, to know that you are better off without him. You are doing very well on your own and you are happy.

A business dress code can be everything to win your case.

You are going into court to win. Dress and act like a winner! Be forceful but respectful.

Thank the Judge and offer your paperwork at the appropriate time. Never interrupt the judge, or your opponent. Just smile and wait your turn. Believe me when your turn comes around, you will have the Judges attention. Present your case in the courtroom, like you were the CEO of a corporation.

5. Situation and Circumstances

You can always change your current situation with drive and determination. The best thing of all is that you can become wealthy or financially secure and your Ex cannot claim a penny if you make them sign off in court first!

Ha...how do you like me now Ex?

Your–In-Laws may not believe all of your problems with their son but eventually at some point he or she will slip up and they will see his faults with their own eyes. Once again remain silent and it will speak for itself in time.

6. Expertise and Knowledge

You have to become a bookworm sometimes in order to get what information you need. Gather as much information as you can on the internet, library and other resources. Join an online notice board for other divorced women. Most of these people have been through the same ordeals and they can help. I'm serious here! Some of these people have incredible stories and solutions.

Most lawyers will offer you a free consultation on your first visit. The phone book is full of them. Look a few up in your neighborhood and pay them all a call. Get free legal advice until you are sure you know what you are doing. Then go down to the courthouse and start filing.

The fees in each state differ but it's usually not too much. Check whether or not the court decides that you and your spouse need to an intermediary, for the sake of the children or not too. That might cost you a little more.

7. Information and Wisdom

The smarter you get the less likely your Ex will ever be able to take advantage of you again, especially in the courtroom where it will really counts the most.

Has the soon to be Ex become unbelievably cruel? As long as you know ahead of the game what to expect then you can at least go into the divorce fighting a fair fight. Knowledge is power.

Your Ex may be throwing flowery stuff and his charm at you about trying to remain good friends for the sake of the children. When in fact he may be secretly preparing to take you for a ride.

These are some of the more common manipulations:

Taking all the money out your joint checking and savings accounts. Get yourself a separate account before you leave him!

Making plans behind your back to out maneuver you in court.

He may be taking notes on you too.

Psychologically, mentally, emotionally trying to break you down.

Crying on your shoulder, that he still loves you to keep you off his back.

Sometimes the Ex will try and make you out to be the bad parent.

If you have to go to mediation over the children do not allow him to pick the psychologist for the kids. He may even try to contact the doctor. He will try to make himself out to be a martyr and smelling like roses before you even get to speak to the doctor yourself.

8. Reward and Final Goal

Figure out really quickly what it is you want the end result to be from your divorce. Some women see divorce as the end of the world.

I have heard "but I still love him and maybe we can still make it work." That's usually going backwards and not looking forward. Just remember why you are here at this point to begin with. You are more than likely missing what is comfortable to you. That is all.

Remember we do become vulnerable all over again, if you allow it into your life. The first thing a lot of people go out and do is find a new love. This is a very big mistake!

9. Find out who you

Someone else may have always told you who were, but that is not really true. A new relationship should only happen when you are completely healed and whole. Then you have a better chance of meeting someone more genuine and compatible.

Spend some time with yourself every day. Thirty minutes is a life saver, so shut the world and family out in that time. Light some candles around the bathtub and sink into it. Don't wallow in self-pity and woe is me for months after you are officially divorced.

You need to begin your life again. This time do it the right way.

Go back to school if you want to. Take a class in fun stuff if that's what you want. Join social groups and make new friends. Get out there and live your life!

10. How to Verbally Destroy your Opponent in Court

Under the Rules Section you are keeping your journal…right?

You are also keeping a written log of all your spouses' bad habits?

You have gathered some credible and exposing information about your spouse. Use all of these bad behaviors into your motions in court.

Expose everything in a way that shows the necessary connections. If it's for custody you want to show yourself as the most responsible and caring parent.

For child support issues, you want to prove to the court why your husband can afford to pay your children more than he currently is. Stay Calm and Composed as you present to the Judge.

11. Do not go overboard

If he is paying support and you are primarily fighting about assets, do not tell the judge he goes to strip joints or nightclubs. There is no reason to intentionally hurt your own financial status, by totally enraging your spouse.

You need only prove the points necessary to your case. If he is not paying his support then the judge needs to know what he is doing with his money. Let the judge know then, what the money is being spent on.

If he is getting more than his fair share of assets the judge needs a very clear and precise breakdown of what assets you each have, and who has what claims, the children, etc.

Always remember that what you put out in public can always come back at you. Court houses keep tons of records and some of these are accessible in the public arena too.

Do not involve your children in the battle. They do not need to see a smear campaign involving their parents. They love you both and it's not fair to put them in the middle.

Chapter 10: Conclusion

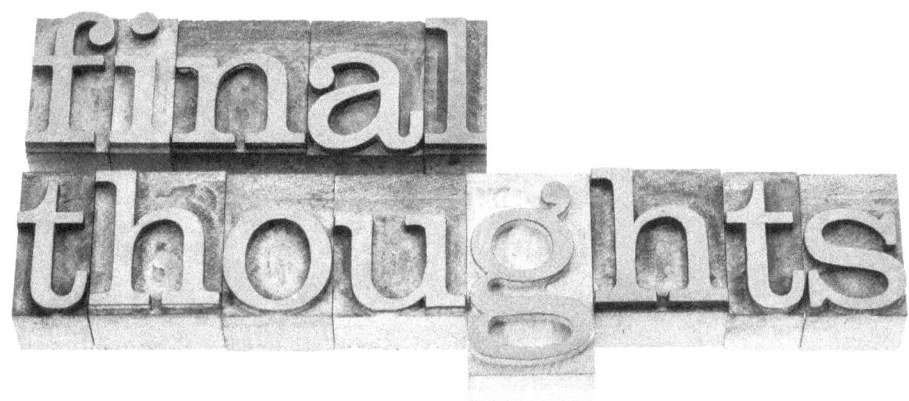

Hopefully this book has enabled you to understand more about the dynamics of divorce and how to achieve your goals with a better outcome.

Each one of us can always choose to be a victim or come out on the other end as a healthier, happier person.

Sometimes guerilla warfare tactics are in order with divorce. It seems in some cases we are left with no other alternative. Whatever decisions you choose to make in the divorce will be because of a good basis of knowledge and understanding.

The goal of this this book was able to equip you with the insights you need to start off on the right foot and stay ahead of the game.

I wish you all the best in your future as a happier and free individual.

Meet the Author

Jane Wymer is known among her friends as "The Matchmaker." It's not just that she has a sense of who will "fit" together, although she definitely does. It's that she's a student of people, and over the years she's gained a lot of wisdom in what makes people datable. She has a kind spirit and is often able to gently help people recognize areas that need some work.

The child of two therapists, Jane has been helping people solve conflict since she could talk. She gave pep talks to stuffed animals and advice to her elementary school teachers. During high school, she observed that while her classmates were obsessing about looks, the thing that really drew people to one another was confidence. She was the person who helped all her friends find—and keep—relationships, but didn't have one of her own. For the longest time she was great at unraveling anyone's love life, but in her own she was the classic over-thinker. When she finally met her husband, Mr. Surely-He-Isn't-Right, his mantra to her was, "Less thinking, more trusting." And it worked!

More Books by Jane Wymer

How to Get Your Ex Back: Win Back Your Ex and Rebuild Your Relationship.

Online Dating: Successful Methods that Work

www.ingramcontent.com/pod-product-compliance
Lightning Source LLC
LaVergne TN
LVHW081545060526
838200LV00048B/2225